P9-DTJ-947

Praying with Our Hands

MCKEON MEMORIAL LIBRARY
ST. PATRICK'S SEMINARY
320 MIDDLEFIELD ROAD
MENLO PARK, CA 94025

DISCARD

126877

Praying with Our Hands

21 PRACTICES OF EMBODIED PRAYER FROM THE WORLD'S SPIRITUAL TRADITIONS

JON M. SWEENEY

photographs by
JENNIFER J. WILSON

foreword by
MOTHER TESSA BIELECKI

afterword by
TAITETSU UNNO, PH.D.

Walking Together, Finding the Way
SkyLight Paths Publishing
Woodstock, Vermont

BL
560
.S94
2000

Praying with Our Hands
Twenty-One Practices of Embodied Prayer
from the World's Spiritual Traditions
© 2000 by SkyLight Paths Publishing

All rights reserved. No part of this book may be reproduced or trans-
mitted in any form or by any means, electronic or mechanical, including photocopying, recording, or by any information storage and
retrieval system, without permission in writing from the publisher.

For information regarding permission to reprint material from this
book, please mail or fax your request in writing to SkyLight Paths
Publishing, Permissions Department, at the address / fax number listed
below.

LIBRARY OF CONGRESS CATALOGING-IN-PUBLICATION DATA

Sweeney, Jon M., 1967–
Praying with our hands : twenty-one practices of embodied prayer
from the world's spiritual traditions / Jon M. Sweeney ; photographs
by Jennifer J. Wilson ; foreword by Tessa Bielecki ; afterword by
Taitetsu Unno.
          p.   cm.
Includes bibliographical references.
ISBN 1-893361-16-0 (pbk.)
1. Prayer. 2. Body, Human—Religious aspects. 3. Hand—Religious
aspects. I. Title.
BL560 .S94 2000
291.4'3—dc21

                                            00-011116

10 9 8 7 6 5 4 3 2 1

Manufactured in Canada
Cover and interior design by Fishman Design

SkyLight Paths, "Walking Together, Finding the Way" and colophon
are trademarks of LongHill Partners, Inc., registered in the U.S.
Patent and Trademark Office.

Walking Together, Finding the Way
Published by SkyLight Paths Publishing
A Division of LongHill Partners, Inc.
Sunset Farm Offices, Route 4, P.O. BOX 237
Woodstock, VT 05091
Tel:(802) 457-4000
Fax:(802) 457-4004
www.skylightpaths.com

For my grandmother,
CLELIA BOSETTI SWEENEY
(1913-1997)

who prayed for me
each day.

And for Danelle,
my love.

Contents

CONTENTS

Foreword

In a series of mystical poems, St. John of the Cross describes Christmas as a wedding: the wedding of God and matter, Divine and human, spirit and flesh. The *Romances* are nowhere near as sublime as John of the Cross's other poetry, but they give us great insight into the role of the body in spiritual practice. And they introduce us to the great mystery known as spiritual marriage or bridal mysticism. Through the poetry of the *Romances*, St. John gives us a whole new image of Christmas. Jesus emerges from his mother's womb not as a helpless baby but as an erotic bridegroom, and the celebration of Christmas becomes a wedding feast, the consummation of a marriage.

Throughout the history of Christianity and other traditions as well, as author Jon Sweeney notes, some have crudely separated the bride and groom and attempted to divorce matter from spirit, body from soul, earth from heaven, as though one were evil and the other good. It is important to remember that this tendency, whatever we call it, has always been not merely criticized, but even condemned by the Christian Church. At her best, the Church has preserved the genuine spirit of Christ, expressed so beautifully by the Carmelite monk William McNamara, who teaches:

> Ever since the Incarnation, when the Word became flesh, no one is permitted to scorn or disregard anything human, natural or earthy, and this includes the body. The Incarnation establishes without a doubt,

once and for all, the *given-ness* of union with God. We do not have to *attain* divine union. We do not have to climb out of our messy flesh into the pure Spirit of God. God has become man. Our flesh is his flesh. Our body is his body.

With this emphasis, it is clear that there can be no spiritual practice where the body does not have a role to play. The body mediates the spirit. "We are on earth and clothed with it," said St. Teresa of Ávila, the sixteenth-century mystic. "We are not angels," she wrote, "but we have a body. To desire to be angels while here on earth is foolishness." Unlike those divisive "heretics" who deny Jesus his humanity, his sensuousness, his sexuality—and therefore deny ours as well—Teresa insists that however spiritual we are, we must not flee from Jesus' corpo-reality, from the flesh, from the body. God isn't satisfied if we merely bring our "souls" to prayer—as if that were even possible—he desires our bodies as well.

How do we do this? Jon Sweeney shows us in this helpful little book, vividly illustrated by twenty-one of Jennifer Wilson's photographs. Many of the world's major religious traditions are represented—Christianity, Judaism, Islam, Hinduism, Buddhism—as well as the lesser-known paths of Shakers, yogis, and Sufis.

We see hands lighting the Sabbath candles, receiving Holy Communion, using a rosary, making the Sign of the Cross, and setting aside sacred space. We see foot washing, the veneration of icons, the beautiful Hindu and Buddhist *mudras* (hand gestures), and the ecstatic turning dance of the Sufis with its deeply symbolic hand movements. Included, too, are examples of prayer in the actions of our ordinary everyday lives: gestures of lovingkindness, of compassion, of righteous protest, of sharing meals, of work as prayer. There are meditations from varied sources: Rumi the Persian and Hafiz the Sufi poet; Rabbi Abraham Joshua Heschel and Mahatma Gandhi; Thich Nhat Hanh and Shunryu Suzuki; the Psalms and the Upanishads, as well as contemporary authors André Dubus and John O'Donohue.

In this work that was inspired more than fifteen years ago, when he first read the works of Thomas Merton, Jon Sweeney has made a valuable contribution. Instead of "reducing the body to a kind of stumbling block to spiritual understanding and nothing more," he shows us that "our bodies can *embody* prayer, or be places where prayer is actively happening. We don't— or shouldn't—just *think* our prayers…. Prayer can involve our bodies as much as our minds," offering us "new ways for celebrating and practicing the sacredness of life." St. Teresa of Ávila would applaud this book.

MOTHER TESSA BIELECKI
NADA HERMITAGE

Acknowledgments

We gratefully acknowledge the many people who helped and contributed in creating the photographs in this book, including: Mary Angelis, John Arida, Rev. Fr. Robert Arida, Susan Arida, Marilyn Cathcart, Rev. Samuel H. Brown, Alice Carter, Jennifer Devine, Rev. William E. Dickerson II, Belynda Dunn, Tamar Enoch, Philip Francis, Mohamed Hassan, Fyodor Kouranov, Elizabeth Kouranova, Susan Kurth, Carl Mastandrea, Rabbi David Meyer, Cory Meyer, Jeremy Meyer, Marla Meyer, Daphne Noyes, Hugh Olmsted, Maria Olmsted, Jeanne Paradise, Scott Paradise, Alexandra Pokrovskaya, Anastasia Pokrovskaya, Eugenia Pomerantzeff, Dr. Roland Shoemaker, Karen Summers, Danelle Sweeney, Chris van Haight, Brother David Vryhof, Rabbi Elaine Zecher, and Lora Zorian.

We also thank the following organizations: the Boston Dawah Committee; the Boston Photo Collaborative; the Cambridge Zen Center; Canterbury Shaker Village, Canterbury, New Hampshire; Concord Baptist Church, Boston; Dignity Boston; the Greater Love Tabernacle, Boston; Holy Trinity Orthodox Cathedral, Boston; Northeastern University; the Islamic Society of Boston; the Seventh-day Adventist Temple, Boston; and the Society of Saint John the Evangelist, Cambridge, Massachusetts.

Praying with Our Hands

Introduction

How Do We Pray with Our Hands?

Prayer is the most universal expression of the presence of God. We express devotion, rage, submission, and many other emotions in prayer. We often plead in prayer. In fact, when the professed nonbeliever pleads in prayer at a time of crisis we may say that she is not really a nonbeliever after all.

We most often think of prayer as something spoken, but it can also be expressed in other ways. What we say, what we do, and how we do it all express God's presence, when we are prayerful.

When asked to picture prayer in terms of where it happens, most people imagine it arising inside them. There is ancient precedent for this. The sixth-century Christian mystic St. Isaac the Syrian wrote: "Enter eagerly into the treasure house that lies within you, and so you will see the treasure house of heaven.... The ladder that leads to the Kingdom is hidden within you." This understanding has been common in many spiritual traditions.

Our modern understanding may be somewhat more literal. We often see prayer as happening like this: An emotion or an idea wells up inside of us that needs words to express it; the emotion or idea somehow transfers to our brain; there we process the language needed to put it into words. We have been conditioned to think that prayer is mostly a mental activity—that it is in some way located in our brains.

There are exceptions, of course. Many of us who pray believe with the psalmist of the Hebrew scriptures that there are times when we cannot articulate our feelings in words—when only sighs are possible. We may experience prayer this way, especially in times of great loss. But even this view of prayer pictures the process in the same way—as a mental process. Our brain either finds the right words for our feelings or ideas, or it doesn't.

Aside from whether or not our feelings, ideas, and brains work this way, this common view of how prayer works does not take into account how our body is involved. We use our bodies to express ourselves in spiritual ways—and these physical expressions can be prayers too. For example, one way to show humility in God's presence is to prostrate oneself, or bow at the waist, or simply bow with the head. Are these expressions any less meaningful than a spoken prayer, such as "Lord, have mercy on me"?

Consider for a moment the statement of the Jewish mystic and theologian Abraham Joshua Heschel, who said of his experience marching with Dr. Martin Luther King, Jr. in Alabama, "My feet were praying." The meaning in our heads can become the meaning in our bodies. When we use our bodies with spiritual intent, both our bodies and the occasion become sacred. Sometimes these bodily actions accompany spoken prayers; sometimes they are prayers in and of themselves.

What Is Embodied Prayer?

In saying "My feet were praying," Heschel meant that our bodies can *embody* prayer, or be places where prayer is actively happening. Our actions and movements can be expressions of prayer to God. We don't—or shouldn't—just *think* our prayers. We can embody the feelings and emotions usually expressed only as spoken or mental prayers in our actions. Prayer can involve our bodies as much as our minds, as we communicate with God, bless, honor, and petition God, rage in the presence of God, and show our devotion. We can show and express with our bodies what we say and express with our minds. This is prayer in motion—and it takes practice. If you try, you can see that prayer can take many forms, and simple actions can have profound meaning in your spiritual life.

When we see prayer as only mental or verbal we can easily become discouraged. Spoken prayers can sometimes feel as if they travel out of us into a void and never come back. When we don't hear a response, what do we do? We may stop praying, feeling, "what's the point?" The problem at these times is that our vision of prayer is too narrow. We are focusing only on the words that are prayed from our minds and forgetting about the life that prays them—our hearts (will) and bodies (actions). We need to realize that God is in us and is part of us. We need to stop talking to God as if we were not intimately one. Embodied prayer is a spiritual practice in which you are able to see your will and actions intermingled with the Divine, engaged together with the world. When you practice embodied prayer, the very motions of your body create meaning for your words like sound creates meaning in poetry.

Many of us have a hard time accepting or expressing embodied prayer because we tend to view our bodies as very personal. For others of us, embodied prayer is as natural as spoken prayer—maybe even more so. To see how you feel with it, try the following exercise:

Imagine the foot-washing ceremony common in some Christian traditions, following the example of Jesus in the Gospels where he washes the feet of his disciples to show the meaning of humility and service. Practice this: Place a large bowl of warm water on the floor in front of your closest friend, or your spouse. Remove her shoes and socks and gently wash her feet in the bowl as an expression of thanking God for her. Caring for the body of your friend is to care for God. (You can think your thankfulness and care in your mind, but focus and practice also expressing it through your hands.) If you find this exercise difficult, simply *imagine* washing someone's feet, or wash the feet of a newborn baby.

If you are like most people, the foot-washing exercise will make you uncomfortable at first. Many cannot do it. Why? Probably in part because we have been conditioned to remove our bodies from the expression of our spiritual selves. We can think and say our love to each other and to God, but we often have difficulty expressing it with our bodies.

The prayerful act of foot-washing is not simply your hands caring for another person's feet, but a prayer to God on behalf of another. It is a prayer performed with your hands. Now, practice washing your own feet with the same spirit, the same caress, as if you are preparing your feet for sacred service, or simply caring for yourself—both can be prayerful acts.

Taming the Body in the Spiritual Traditions

Though the spiritual traditions are rich with ways of involving the body in prayer (as the twenty-one examples in this book demonstrate), we are still sometimes prone to focusing on those practices that limit prayer to mental or vocal expression.

Because many spiritual practices aim to bring the body under control, there can be a temptation to regard the body as a hindrance rather than as our ally in attaining our spiritual goals. Some meditation techniques, for instance, use the body to master control of the mind. These techniques include focusing the mind on the sensation of breathing out and breathing in, or focusing the eyes on the flame of a candle, or repeating a mantra with total concentration in order to quiet what is called "monkey mind"—the out-of-control thinking created by the flood of external stimuli we face each day. Techniques like these focus on stilling the body to make room in the mind for true concentration and awareness—again, mostly mental processes. These forms of meditation focus on spiritual awareness happening primarily in our brains.

A pervasive tendency in traditional religion, and throughout much of the history of philosophy, has been toward trying to free oneself from the body's impassioned thoughts and feelings in order to lead the mind, heart, and soul—whatever is left when the body is effectively "removed"—to a purer knowledge of the Divine. The idea: The inapprehensible mysteries of God are hidden in the world or in me, and my body will not help me discover them. With this kind of thinking as our inheritance, it is easy to see how we can be led to focus on the mind at the expense of the body.

The Eastern religions are not immune to this tendency. One of the four great vows of Zen is: "However inexhaustible the passions are, I vow to extinguish them." Enlightenment is achieved in Zen when we truly open the mind's eye, discovering our real nature. Similarly, a Jain prayer entreats: "O God, help me to victory over myself, for difficult to conquer is oneself, though when that is conquered, all is conquered." This "self" to be conquered is sometimes viewed as the body and what it represents.

This perspective is common in the history of Christian spirituality too. One of the original emphases of Christian monasticism was to separate from the world in order to wage a personal war on evil—both within us and around us. Saint Benedict's (d. 547) *Rule* for monks includes a list of seventy-two "Instruments of Good Works," among them: "To chastise the body" and "To despise one's own will." Though Christian monastic spirituality is replete with practices of embodied prayer, there remains a tendency for Christians to see the body as an enemy.

Another word of advice frequently encountered in various faiths has to do with blocking the phenomena or external stimuli we perceive with our senses from reaching our hearts and minds. If we refuse to allow our hearts and minds to engage with what our senses unavoidably encounter, so the advice goes, our spiritual lives will be unencumbered to pursue God. In the Eastern Christian tradition, this is sometimes called practicing *watchfulness:* "Watchfulness...is the heart's stillness and, when free from mental images, it is the guarding of the intellect."

For centuries, Christian mystics have emphasized viewing the body as something to subdue as much as possible in order to approach the unity and purity of the Godhead. The Christian mystics speak of practicing *detachment*, which frees us from the world—and the body—in order to focus us on God alone. The fourteenth-century German mystic Meister Eckhart says: "This you must know for sure: when the free mind is quite detached, it constrains God to itself, and if it were able to stand formless and free of all accidentals, it would assume God's proper nature." The founder of the Jesuit society, Ignatius Loyola, similarly advised his followers in the practice "of contemplation, of vocal and mental prayer, and [a] way of preparing and disposing the soul to rid itself of all inordinate attachments, and, after their removal, of seeking and finding the will of God."

When properly understood, all of these practices are of inestimable value. But the problem is that they have a history of being misunderstood. They have too often been taken outside their proper context, to be seen as reducing the body to a kind of stumbling block to spiritual understanding and nothing more. By subjugating our bodies and diligently quieting all that is experienced by our senses, we may hope to become like those of whom Jesus spoke when he said: "Blessed are the pure in heart, for they shall see God" (Matthew 5:8). This assumption of how prayer works lives deep inside many of us who pray.

But embodied prayer is different. With embodied prayer our bodies—even our hands—can be used to express our devotion to God, often very simply and ordinarily, apart from words—or most powerfully when combined with words. In embodied prayer, our physical actions are expressions of ourselves—God in us—often apart from what we might be thinking or saying. Our bodies can teach us as much as our minds can. In embodied prayer, the thought (mind), will (heart), and actions (body) all come together. Our prayers involve our whole being or person; we are complete spiritual organisms when we practice prayer this way.

Our Hands Can Make Prayer Visible

> Where you put your foot on earth, my life,
> Tulips, violets, and jasmine sprout.
> If you take some clay and breathe on it,
> It becomes a hawk, a dove, a crow!
> If you wash your hand in earthen bowls
> They become, thanks to your hand, pure gold.
>
> —RUMI

For many of us, practicing embodied prayer involves a shift in perspective. We begin to imagine our spiritual lives differently, with a more holistic vision. New ways for celebrating and practicing the sacredness of life will open up for you as you begin on this path. You will see how everyday actions can be prayerful expressions to God. You will also see how religious ritual is rich with prayer of the body, and how expressive just your hands can become.

Imagine the many emotions your hands already express: They can invite or beckon, repel or reject, hide or reveal, console or protect; they can embrace. When we pray with our hands we are enfleshing the sacred—not just talking to God, or focusing our minds. In our hands, prayer becomes visible.

Mahatma Gandhi said: "Worship and prayer...are not to be

performed with the lips but with the heart. That is why they can be performed equally by the dumb and stammerer, by the ignorant and stupid." Praying with our hands shows how prayer is for everyone.

Compiled here are twenty-one examples from people's lives in the world's spiritual traditions that show praying with hands, in word and image. People in every major religious tradition—including Christianity, Judaism, Islam, Hinduism and Buddhism—pray with their hands. Several lesser-known spiritual paths, too—like those of the Shakers, the yogis, and the Sufis—are also represented here. No matter what your background is, you can use these examples to envision your prayer life differently and to find ways you can pray with your hands. Don't leave these words and photographs flat on the pages of this book—use them.

Before you begin to consciously practice praying with your hands, you may want to perform this simple exercise: Extend your hands with palms upward, a gesture of openness to the Divine, and as a gift of your hands to the Source of Life.

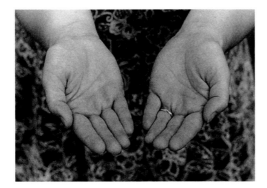

Work as Prayer

As we bend our bodies to a task, in that bending our bodies and the task become sacred.

Mother Ann Lee, founder of the Shakers, was an inspiring and quixotic leader. One of her most important teachings was, like all Shaker work, beautiful in its simplicity: "Hands to work, hearts to God." There are no menial tasks in a world where everything is sacred. Each task is an occasion for us to practice the presence of God. That was the role of a Shaker in the world. How would this simple saying and practice transform your work?

> The chambers of thy soul expand,
> And stretch thy tents abroad;
> Clasp Labor in Religion's hand
> And aid the work of God.
> —SHAKER HYMN

Welcoming the Sabbath

God's light infuses all of creation. It is our responsibility to release it in everyday, ordinary ways. Then, we will see more clearly the world to come.

"The Sabbath is a mirror of the world to come," according to the *Zohar*, the primary text of Kabbalah, the general term for Jewish mysticism, stemming from the Hebrew word "to receive" or "to welcome." A remembrance of the Exodus from Egypt and a reminder of the work of creation, the Sabbath is welcomed by lighting Sabbath candles. God's first act of creation was when God said, "Let there be light."

Jews celebrate the coming of the Sabbath at home on Friday evening, marking it as the beginning of a holy day. Traditionally, a Jewish woman lights two candles just before the Sabbath begins—when the first two stars can be seen in the sky—to welcome this holy day. Some people light additional candles for their children or grandchildren. *Shabbat* reminds us of our role in the ongoing work of creation, as we release the light of God infused in all things through our own efforts to "repair the world."

> Creation, we are taught, is not an act that happened once upon a time, once and forever. The act of bringing the world into existence is a continuous process…. Every instant is an act of creation.
>
> —ABRAHAM JOSHUA HESCHEL

31

Accepting the Holy Eucharist

We feed on God in our hearts by faith when we hunger for righteousness.

It began, of course, when Jesus observed the traditional Passover meal with his disciples before the crucifixion. Centuries of Christian ceremony have turned one simple Passover meal into the celebration of the Holy Eucharist—a remembrance of Christ's death.

In many Anglican and Catholic traditions, a priest recites from the liturgy: "The Gifts of God for the People of God. Take them in remembrance that Christ died for you, and feed on him in your hearts by faith, with thanksgiving."

"Feed on him in your hearts"—what powerful religious language, most likely missed by many observants amid the three-thousand-or-so—word rite. However, wherever this memorial of Christian redemption is practiced, you will usually see true hunger on the faces of a few present—hungering after God.

When the priest places the host in the palm of my hand, I put it in my mouth and taste and chew and swallow the intimacy of God.

—ANDRÉ DUBUS

Welcoming the Deity

You don't need to travel far to find spiritual insight. When we direct our gaze inward, yogis teach, we commune with the Divine. It is only because our everyday lives distract us that we do not live in God-consciousness all the time.

Many yoga techniques—like the simple and familiar *anjali-mudra* ("welcoming the deity") hand position—say with our hands what inwardly we feel: "I want to know You!"

Practicing yoga is all about surrender and letting go, allowing the body to find its center in our supreme Self. In that center is the Divine, the Divine in all of us.

The supreme Self is neither born nor dies.
Cannot be grasped, cannot be seen.
—ATMA UPANISHAD

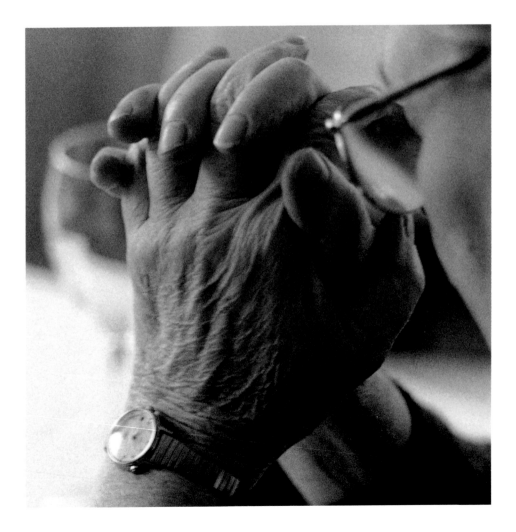

Table Grace

Ordinary moments of thankfulness can deepen a personal friendship with God over time. Repetition naturally breeds familiarity.

Perhaps the most familiar posture of prayer in the Christian world is the bowed head, closed eyes, and folded hands in saying a *table grace*—a blessing on the food about to be eaten in thankfulness to God as Source and Giver of all things.

We often become disinterested in repetitive forms of prayer— repeating the same words and holding the same posture each time out of habit or a sense of obligation. But there is something inherently good in the repetition: Through repeated actions the body can train the heart in love and devotion.

Performing the ordinary event of a table grace often raises poignant memories—of a devout grandparent's hands, for instance, gently clasped beneath a bowed head, as if a private friendship is engaged at that moment.

Let my prayer arise in Thy sight as incense,
And let the lifting up of my hands be an evening sacrifice.
—PSALM 141:2

There is an astonishing vastness
of movement and life
emanating sound and light
from my folded hands.
—HAFIZ

Resisting Evil

Wherever there is evil in the world, there is the potential for good. It is our responsibility to transform it.

Abraham Joshua Heschel spoke of the ways in which God is no longer at home in the Creation because we act as if God doesn't exist. Instead of being divine agents as we should, we effectively remove God from the world with our inaction. Heschel says: "To pray means to bring God back into the world.... To pray means to expand God's presence."

We pray with our bodies when we put them in front of tanks. We pray with our hands when we link arms together to fight injustice. We are co-creators with the Divine when we resist evil. The world is more sacred at these moments.

Praying with Icons

Worship spaces usually have special spiritual significance because of the symbols of the Divine presence there. In Taoist and Hindu temples, incense symbolizes Divine manifestations. In Roman Catholic churches, the presence of the Holy Eucharist is the presence of God. In synagogues, the Torah scroll instills special reverence. We show love and devotion when we adore what represents or points to God. In the Orthodox Christian tradition, icons are symbolic representations of the holy, usually images of Christ or of the saints. Venerating them brings the body into the act of prayer. One common gesture is to kiss the hand and to touch that kiss to the icon in prayer. Our hands show reverence for life when we practice the presence of God.

> God is not an idea and praying is not an exercise to improve our idea of God, though for those of us who have spent a good deal of our lives in classrooms, it can be difficult to get beyond the world of ideas. Prayer is the cultivation of the awareness of God's actual presence.
>
> —JIM FOREST,
> *Praying with Icons*

The Cosmic Mudra

In *zazen* ("sitting" meditation), posture is important—and this includes the hands. After describing in detail how the hands should be positioned to form the cosmic mudra, the great Zen teacher Shunryu Suzuki says: "You should keep this universal mudra with great care, as if you were holding something very precious in your hand."

We are inundated with attachments—our feelings, insecurities, friends and family members, our stories. They all have their places in our lives, but ultimately, as Zen teaches, we have to let go of every one of these treasures.

When we successfully let go of the treasures in our lives, we awaken to see the meaning behind the mystery of life, the greatest treasure of all. This is symbolized by the cosmic mudra—holding the treasure that cannot be held—"the jewel in the hand, opening endlessly."

Laying on of Hands

People have gathered together as religious communities for millennia because we need each other in order to understand God and ourselves. Like babies, we need to be touched—by each other and the Divine—in order to grow.

In Protestant traditions, members of the community needing special care, such as healing or counsel, or those about to enter into positions of authority and special responsibility, receive a blessing accompanied by the touch of many supporting hands. These hands are meant to be the "hands" of God.

One of the beautiful Protestant hymns, written at the turn of the last century, says:

Open my eyes, that I may see
glimpses of truth you have for me;
place in my hands the wonderful key
that shall unlock and set me free.

Silently now, on bended knee,
ready I wait your will to see;
open my eyes, illumine me,
Spirit divine!
                                        —CLARA H. SCOTT

Dancing with God

Spiritual devotion can be similar to the love between lovers. We can yearn for the Divine like a lover yearns for his beloved—desiring to be absorbed by her. But ultimately we cannot see or touch the object of our spiritual passion.

The mystical movements of Hinduism, Hasidism, and Sufism teach us that union with God is not only possible, but also natural to our human condition. Those traveling these mystical paths sometimes express a blissful joy and the intensity of this relationship through dance, expressing our union of body and spirit with the Spirit in all bodies.

In Sufi dance, or "turning," the *dervish* becomes a doorway through which the Divine and human meet. Receiving energy from God with the right hand turned toward heaven, she returns energy to the earth through her left hand.

> Draw me in your footsteps, let us run.
> The king has brought me into his rooms;
> You will be our joy and our gladness.
> We shall praise your love more than wine;
> How right it is to love you.
> —SONG OF SONGS, 1:4

Breaking Bread

All things contain a shard of God's goodness, which is why sustenance for the body can also be nourishment for the soul. The stages for making bread are often metaphors for steps on the spiritual path: Planting, sowing, harvesting, kneading, rising, sharing. Breaking bread is a simple gesture of sharing a meal, but in spiritual traditions it can mean much more.

Hospitality is a spiritual practice when we are prepared to show God's goodness to each other at any moment. Common to all religious traditions is the idea of welcoming a stranger at our table. By preparing our hearts we will be able to respond with our hands to the needs we see around us, sharing God's goodness in simple ways.

A piece of bread contains a cloud. Without a cloud, the wheat cannot grow. So when you eat the piece of bread, you eat the cloud, you eat the sunshine, you eat the minerals, time, space, everything.

—THICH NHAT HANH

Counting Prayers

We use many images and metaphors for the spiritual life, from ascending a divine ladder to descending into a sacred well. Each speaks to our striving for connections to the Divine—one of the reasons why we pray.

Sometimes a simple, unbroken chain of beads or knots—called prayer beads, malas, or rosaries—devoutly used, cannot only help to focus our attention in prayer, but to create a circle of intimate relationship with the object of our prayer.

This practice has ancient origins. Paul the Hermit, a fourth-century Christian monk, decided to pray three hundred times each day and used pebbles to focus his intention, throwing one aside with each prayer. The early followers of Muhammad created strings of thirty-three, sixty-six, and ninety-nine beads with which to pray the names of Allah. Similarly, Hindu devotees of the god Shiva, as well as Buddhists, use a strand of 108 beads. Other early contemplatives used string, tying one knot for each prayer. Orthodox Christian monks still tie strings of 100 knots called *chotki* (Russian) or *komvoskoini* (Greek)—each knot is complicated and rich with symbolism.

St. Teresa of Ávila called the rosary "a chain uniting heaven and earth." Mystics in many traditions have regarded prayer beads with similar importance. As our hands make their way around the strand, we—and our prayers—are woven into the fabric of the Divine.

Daily Honor

Many religious traditions practice a daily regimen of repeated prayer—but none combines the spiritual with the physical like *Salat*, Muslim daily prayer. According to tradition, "The Prayer" was first taught to the prophet Muhammad by angels, and it mirrors their constant adoration of God.

Salat is practiced all over the globe—five times daily the Islamic world faces Mecca and praises: "In the name of Allah, boundlessly merciful and compassionate!" The beloved Sufi poet Hafiz (fourteenth century) sings:

I bow to God in gratitude,
And I find the moon is also busy
Doing the same.

The Prayer has several stages and universes of meaning: standing, bowing, prostrating, and kneeling all use the hands to recognize and praise Allah ("God" in Arabic) in humility and devotion.

A mosque is unnecessary for *Salat*—the inner sanctum, or the prayerful heart, is the place where the prayer begins (and on a portable prayer mat). Our bodies are the true mosques, churches, synagogues, and temples—when we use them as places for daily honor to God.

Foot Washing

The Hebrew scriptures tell of times when Abraham and others offered water to their guests that they might wash their feet after a long journey—foot washing as hospitality. Muslim and Jewish traditions teach ablutions, or foot washing as ritual cleansing—occasions for turning from the world and preparing for awareness of God.

There are many reasons to wash our bodies, and often we are reminded of our need for spiritual cleansing, as well.

In the Christian tradition there is a little-known ceremony that centers on a different kind of foot washing. It is an act of servitude, imitating Christ on the night before his crucifixion when he washed the feet of his disciples.

This act of the hands can show us how humility requires practice— it doesn't come naturally. Imagine the astonishment of Jesus' twelve disciples when he knelt at their feet to perform this act reserved for servants! How might this spirit transform our leaders today? Simple gestures can change the world.

Showing Compassion

Modern life can be deceptive, making us think and feel as if we are no longer intimately connected to the world around us. Buddhism teaches that the differences we perceive between people are illusory—our vision is flawed.

Central to Buddhist spiritual practice is service to others. Bodhisattvas (Sanskrit for "awakening being") are people who put aside their own striving toward enlightenment in order to help other people reach their own enlightenment. You don't have to be schooled in the *dharma* (Buddha's teachings) to be a bodhisattva—Mother Teresa, Gandhi, Rachel Carson, and Dr. Martin Luther King, Jr. are a few modern examples often cited.

Similarly, central in Judaism is the concept of *tikkun olam*, "repairing the world"; *karma* yoga is another path of selfless service to others; and the life and message of St. Francis of Assisi represents the Christian tradition of taking literally the words of Jesus: "Take nothing for your journey—no staff, nor bag, nor bread, nor money" (Luke 9:3).

All of these paths show how we gain wisdom and compassion through selflessness, when our hands act in the perfect understanding that you are me and that we are One.

Making an Altar

The Hebrew scriptures tell us that, following the great flood, Noah built the first altar, a raised structure for worship to the Most High. Still common in religious ceremonies, altars are used in both public and personal ways.

In Latter-day Saints temples, for example, man and woman kneel at an altar to make their covenant with each other and God in marriage. In addition to these public uses, increasingly common today are home altars, or home shrines, as they are called in Jainism—an assemblage of personal objects that remind one of God, or of things that symbolize Divine blessings.

The home altar can be our set-aside place for honoring the Holy One, and blessing God's guidance and goodness. We can use our hands to create a sacred place that shows the Divine as we know it.

The Sign of the Cross

Christian monks chant the divine office (communal daily prayer) eight times daily in order to follow the Apostle Paul's instruction to "pray without ceasing," and in the words of St. Basil of Caesarea (fourth century), "to imitate on earth the choruses of the angels." They are also doing what in Latin is called *Opus Dei*, "the work of God." It is not just that Christian contemplatives see *themselves* as doing God's work, but that *God* is doing a good work—accomplishing sacred intentions—through our faithful prayers. We never know how this is possible, or often when it happens, but we trust and pray.

Many of the ritual acts of our spiritual lives are performed simply out of reverence, not with the expectation of receiving anything. The Christian's up-and-down, side-to-side movement of the hand in making the sign of the cross has ancient origins—marking the heart and soul in devotion to God in Christ. Gestures like this have the power to form a life around their simple reverence, training us in our capacities for deeper faith, enduring hope, and Divine love.

Practicing Lovingkindness

For many of us, the most difficult obstacle to overcome in spiritual practice is our fear of silence. It is difficult, for instance, to find a place where you can stand for fifteen minutes without hearing a non-natural sound. And if you try it, you may even find that you've become so used to the "comfort" of noise that prolonged periods of quiet make you uncomfortable.

Too much noise and too little silence combine to desensitize us in many ways. But when we practice becoming more aware of the spiritual, we engage with the world around us even in simple, seemingly inconsequential ways. These actions show our spirit.

The Buddhist tradition teaches that it is important to cultivate lovingkindness. To do this, we change how we treat people, animals, and all things. We direct love and compassion their way. This means handling objects gently, avoiding loud speech, and refraining from roughness of all kinds. Our spirit is in our hands.

The practice of touching things deeply on the horizontal level gives us the capacity to touch God.... We can touch the noumenal world by touching the phenomenal world deeply.
—THICH NHAT HANH

Receiving the Spirit

A world of divine possibilities surrounds us at all times. Amid the uncertainties of daily life that sometimes worry and scare us we often discover a deep sacredness underneath it all. We shouldn't really be surprised, but we usually are.

Many religious traditions express this mysterious Divine-human inter- action in very personal terms. The Pentecostal tradition in Christianity teaches how a personal openness to God's will brings an indwelling of special gifts of the Spirit of God. This is, literally, God living in and through us. We can express this openness through our hands—showing our willingness to receive the coming of God into our lives.

Lift up your hands in the holy place
and bless the Lord,
the Lord who made heaven and earth.
—PSALM 134:2

Holy Water

Water has always had mystical meanings for people. The early Greek philosophers believed that the earth was like a disc, around which flowed a great river on all sides.

Most religious traditions use washing in water as a personal means of preparing ceremonially for prayer, meditation, or spiritual service. These ritual cleansings are symbols of our need for spiritual cleanliness—expressed through our hands.

One of these beautiful practices is the Hindu's devotion to Ganga, the goddess of the Ganges, India's most sacred river. Once a heavenly tributary, according to tradition, for millions the Ganges is a sacred place for daily physical and spiritual cleansing. Outside India, Hindus bathe in the spirit of Ganga, in water set aside for this purpose.

In Catholic tradition, water is sanctified by a priest and used for personal and community worship, sometimes sprinkled on worshippers, or simply touched upon entering a sacred place.

Consecrating ourselves with holy water can be a way to signify a separation from the things that deceive, or sully, us as we enter a sacred place. Sometimes a touch can help to restore our spiritual focus.

Passing the Peace

In many ways, often despite our best intentions, our lives are meanderings toward and away from the Divine. It is easy to lose focus.

Our ancient and medieval mothers and fathers viewed this feature of spiritual life in terms of a journey. Wandering in the wilderness with Moses, the Great Going Forth of the Buddha from his father's palace—these are stories we can relate to as spiritual wanderers. Today's pilgrims are the migratory hunters of ancient, past generations.

In our seeking, there is not an object to be found. What we search for, and what we often find, are reminders of our wholeness in God.

In Catholic and Anglican traditions, people at worship express the peace of God to each other with a simple handshake, embrace or kiss, and the words: "The peace of the Lord." Similarly, at the conclusion of *Salat*, the Muslim daily prayer, the devoted often embrace each other with the words, "May the peace of God be upon you."

We can show each other the presence of God with our hands.

Embodied Prayer Is an Expression of Who We Really Are

> Human hands are powerful images. Hands painted the roof on the Sistine Chapel and the heavenly women on the wall of Sigeria, wrote the *Paradiso*, sculpted the *David*; the whole history of our presence on earth could be gleaned from the witness and actions of hands.
>
> —JOHN O'DONOHUE

As the previous twenty-one practices of embodied prayer show, the presence of God is not only to be found in the quiet stillness of our souls, but in the activity of our hands. Gestures and actions like these can help to deepen spiritual life.

When we act in prayer we are most authentically ourselves: Our bodies and minds are in sync, expressing the same intention, expressing ourselves as spiritual agents. We are beings whose true nature is mysteriously one with God. As a poet uses sound to create meaning deeper than the simple definition of words, we can use the motions of our bodies to create deeper meaning in prayer.

The genesis of this little book occurred more than fifteen years ago when I first read the works of Thomas Merton, the Trappist monk and author of *The Seven Storey Mountain.* In the 1960s, when Merton was in his fifties, he started on a new path of spiritual seeking. He looked to the religious traditions of the East, and they changed how he practiced his Christianity. At this time of discovery in Merton's life he met a young Buddhist monk named Thich Nhat Hanh, who was traveling in the U.S. speaking out on the injustices and horror taking place in his homeland of Vietnam. Here were two monks of different traditions, each engaged with the world.

When Merton asked Thich Nhat Hanh what he had learned in his first year in the monastery, Nhat Hanh replied: "How to open and close doors quietly." This struck Merton—and it still strikes me today—as a profound insight into our spiritual lives. This young Buddhist monk was not consumed with studying great texts or memorizing chants and liturgies (although, of course, he had done that too). He wasn't focusing on becoming a spiritual master. He was practicing his faith with his thought (mind), will (heart), and actions (body)—with his life, and he was doing it in little, ordinary ways.

Thich Nhat Hanh's Buddhist tradition teaches that it is important to cultivate mindfulness in everyday life—becoming aware at every moment of the spiritual meaning in things and in our actions. In many ways, mindfulness is what most spiritual practices aim to realize. You don't have to be a Buddhist to live a life marked by mindfulness.

Praying with our hands is a way of practicing mindfulness. It can give stability to our spiritual lives. At times when it is difficult to keep our minds focused in prayer, our hands can train the body's attention and focus the heart's intention. When words don't say adequately what we mean, our hands might be able to show it.

William Butler Yeats said: "The proud and careless notes live on [of 'mouths that speak'] / But bless our hands that ebb away."

You may want to create new ways of hand-prayer in your spiritual life, finding ways that show the meaning of your prayers the best. Better yet, examine your life for opportunities that may be present already. You may discover situations where a new awareness, or a change of vision or perspective, is all that is needed to create meaningful moments of embodied prayer. Other practices that may be new to you, like breaking bread (pp. 48–49), lovingkindness (pp. 62–63), and resisting evil (pp. 38–39) can be cultivated within any spiritual tradition and require no specific skills or religious beliefs.

In all, praying with your hands—or at least beginning to see your body as a place where prayer is embodied—is a path to a more active, sensuous, and dynamic spiritual life. Hafiz says:

I offer my clapping spirit to you,
That is in eternal movement.
Hafiz offers to bow at your feet
With hands that God has shaped and pounded.
Look into my palms, my dear,
They now contain your face and infinite existence.

By praying with your hands you may become mindful with more than your mind, as you practice a prayerful spirit throughout everyday life.

Afterword

When prayer is not simply petitionary or mental, it involves one's whole being—mind, body and spirit, the conscious and unconscious. This embodied prayer is expressed by the hands that worship, whether it be the palms pressed together, hands folded and fingers interlocking, or opened to the sky and earth.

Among the various parts of the human body, the hands have been regarded as expressive of a vast range of human emotions from invitation to rejection, grief to anger, generosity to miserliness, benediction to condemnation, possession to power. Hands have been central to healing and blessing, exorcism and magic, religious ritual and worship. In fact, they are even attributed to the workings of anthropomorphic deities in varied religious traditions.

In spite of differences in the doctrines and practices of world religions, embodied prayer plays a central role in all of them. The unity in diversity is explicit in the somatic expressions of faith, symbolized by the hands in prayer, that may further the interreligious dialogues popular today among Buddhists, Christians, Muslims, Jews, and Hindus.

Although we tend to think of the hands as "parts" of the body, they are in fact no mere appendages; they *embody* the whole human person. The highest form of religiosity and spirituality is found in our hands working together in the worship of the Other. The Cartesian split of body and mind has no place in embodied prayer, for it involves mind, body and spirit, as well as intellect, emotion and will.

The hands in prayer have an even greater significance for all of life, for it overcomes the duality inherent in human thinking and language. That is, thinking involves analysis, the separation of reality into compartments; and language is constructed with words that are artificial constructs that people mistake for reality.

What this means is placed in context by Robert Murphy in his *Overture to Social Anthropology:*
In structural theory the structure of the psyche is universally the same and the working of the mind involves a continual process of sorting one's perceptions into paired opposites, which are then reconciled.... The stream of consciousness becomes broken up into discrete events and things, which are usually reducible to words. [They] allow us to break up reality and reduce it to the hard, objective status of the word. At the same time, it does certain violence to the human grasp of reality—the same mind that sets up these oppositions is also continually trying to mend them, to reconcile them, and to synthesize their antithesis.

When the two hands exist separately and work independently of each other, we have the duality of good and evil, right and wrong, pure and impure, beautiful and ugly, long and short, up and down, high and low, ad infinitum. This forms the basis of a common belief among many cultures that the left hand is inferior and secondary to the right hand; in fact, in some cultures it is considered unclean. The Latin *dextra* is related to the right hand ("dexterous"), and *sinistra* to the left hand ("sinister").

But when the two come together and work in harmonious unison, the wholeness of the spirit becomes manifest. On the everyday level it appears when we place our hands together in saying grace before meals, bow before an altar or religious icon, and form the mudra, usually the left hand over the right, in Zen meditation. The psychological implications are even greater.

When the hands work together, it unifies the bipolarity of the unconscious and conscious, light and darkness, left and right brains. A kind of life energy is engendered that makes the wholeness vibrant. This energy is the *qi* or *ch'i* cultivated in Chinese yogic exercises, as exemplified in such popular movements as qigong and in manuals such as *The Secret of the Golden Flower.* This energy shares some commonality with the healing process involved in the laying on of hands.

This union of opposites also appears in ambidexterity. In the Japanese art of tea ceremony, for example, both the right and left hands of the host preparing a cup of tea must move with the same smooth spontaneity, free of tension and calculation. Neither side is to be favored. And in the martial art of Aikido, which teaches only spherical defensive movements, both the left and right hands are trained to be equally effective, the balance creating a tremendous force coming from the ocean of *qi* at the pit of the stomach.

As the somatic expression of a wide range of sentiments—penitence, supplication, praise, thanksgiving—the hands attain their ultimate sophistication in the language of *mudra*, the symbolic hand gestures that express the highest principles of the religious life, principles that escape discursive thought and verbal representations.

Three images from world religions underscore the centrality of the hands in human affairs. First is the creation of Adam scene in the Sistine Chapel, the famous painting by Michelangelo; second is the figure of Shiva as Nataraja, Lord of Dance, with one hand raised holding the flame of destruction and the other raised in the mudra of fearlessness, inviting all to join the cosmic dance; and third is the Bodhisattva of Constant Bowing in the *Lotus Sutra* who with palms together bowed before every sentient being endowed with Buddha-nature without exception. Shunryu Suzuki in his *Zen Mind, Beginner's Mind* practiced this in everyday life:

> Bowing is a very serious practice. You should be prepared to bow, even in your last moment. Even though it is impossible to get rid of our self-centered desires, we have to do it. Our true nature wants us to…. Sometimes the disciple bows to the master, sometimes the master bows to the disciple. A master who cannot bow to a disciple cannot bow to the Buddha. Sometimes master and disciple bow together to the Buddha. Sometimes we may bow to cats and dogs.

TAITETSU UNNO
JILL KER CONWAY PROFESSOR OF RELIGON EMERITUS
SMITH COLLEGE

Photographer's Notes

When I was first asked to do the photographs for *Praying with Our Hands,* I had several reservations, one of which was a concern that I would not be able to get the results I wanted in photographing people and communities with whom I had no real relationship. In the past, most of my work has been done in the context of the community that I know best, Holy Trinity Orthodox Cathedral in Boston, Massachusetts. Since this is my parish, I know most of the people, the order of the services, the events that form the cycle of life of the parish. I believe that my best photographs come from my direct experience. If the photographer insists on remaining a bystander, it will be apparent in the photograph. But for this project, which involved people and communities with whom I had no preexisting relationship, being a bystander was unavoidable in some ways. I visited a number of different houses of worship in the Boston area for this project, and I also observed a number of ways that people pray outside of churches, synagogues, and mosques. Most of the photographs in this book are a result of those visits and experiences.

To overcome my status as bystander I tried as much as possible to attend to what was happening, not just look for "the shot." I know from the experience of taking photographs in my own parish that during the best of worship and prayer we are transfigured. We arrive as men and women and children caught up in the bustle of the world, persons weighed down by concerns and necessity. The act of worship and prayer requires us to change the focus of our heart, soul, and body from ourselves and our problems to worshiping and praising God. In this change of focus—this change of orientation—we can become transfigured. It was my hope to get a glimpse of this transfiguration for the photographs for this book. This meant that in the brief time that I was in each situation, I tried to be as alert as possible to the activity and "feeling" of the community at worship.

With one minor exception, I used my 35mm Leica range finder, which is entirely manual, without a flash, for all of the shoots. In order to make up for lighting, since I was not using a flash, I used a fast film and overdeveloped it. I also decided early on that I would do all of the film processing myself, because I knew that with the lighting challenges I would be able to adjust development myself with much more flexibility that way. I tried as much as possible to sneak around almost invisibly, encouraging people to go on with what they were doing, and to ignore me and my camera; this was more easily done with a quiet camera without flash. The best of my photographs have a focal point of light that somehow works to illuminate the rest of the image by helping to bring out the detail in the shadows, while always drawing the eye to the light. Thus, I had to be alert to where the natural light was falling and take advantage of it.

The most exciting shoots for me were those where the people completely ignored me in the context of the prayer and worship that were going on. The images that resulted in these situations are much more alive for me. There were other shoots that we arranged with individuals who allowed us to photograph them while they were praying—outside any group context—and the images that resulted from these were also quite satisfying, since I found that people were indeed able to pray even with a photographer present.

A few shoots stand out for me. At the mosque of the Islamic Society of Boston, although I was allowed into the men's section to take pictures during *salat,* the five-times-daily prayer, the image here was actually taken after the formal prayer time was finished. It is a posture of supplication, and only a few of the men prayed in this manner that day—the light falling on the edges of the man's hands and arms really enlivens this image. When I photographed the Mevlevi *dervish* Lora Zorian doing the Sufi "turn," the challenges were manifold-lighting—photographing a fast-moving subject at a slow shutter speed—and yet almost every frame came out in focus, and her photograph is for me the most satisfying in the book. The photograph of "Passing the Peace" was the only image that was usable from my shoot at the Catholic Liturgy that day, which happens sometimes, but it is a little scary when it does. This one brought together all of the elements we wanted to show. Finally, the photographs that I took during worship where I had to muster up the courage to jump into the fray of events—especially the "Foot Washing," "Laying on of Hands," and "Receiving the Spirit"—were rewarding for me because I felt I was able to break the personal barrier of being an outsider and capture the spirit of the moment.

For a photographer, the shoot is not over until the film is successfully developed. Every time I rolled film onto a spool to develop it, I would be praying for successful results, especially for the negatives of events that could not be easily repeated. Pulling a well-done roll of negatives off of the spool is always a thrill for me. After that, one of the most exciting aspects of photography is watching an image emerge in the developer—the interplay of the black and the white creating what you hope will be a delight to the eyes. Added to this excitement was the tension of knowing that getting a chance to repeat a shoot would be difficult in the short amount of time we had to finish the book.

Ultimately, watching each of the photographs come together into a body of work, reflecting the diverse world of prayer and worship that is found all around us, was extremely satisfying.

JENNIFER J. WILSON

Source Notes

Page 19: St. Isaac the Syrian in *The Art of Prayer: An Orthodox Anthology*, translated by E. Kadloubovsky & E. M. Palmer, edited by Timothy Ware (Boston: Faber & Faber, 1997), 164.

Page 24, first paragraph: George Appleton, ed., *The Oxford Book of Prayer* (New York: Oxford University Press, 1985), 908.

Page 24, second paragraph: Anthony C. Meisel and M. L. del Mastro, trans., *The Rule of St. Benedict* (New York: Image Books, 1975), 52–54.

Page 24, third paragraph: St. Hesychios the Priest, "On Watchfulness and Holiness," in *The Philokalia*, vol. 1, translated by G. E. H. Palmer, Philip Sherrard, and Kallistos Ware (Boston: Faber & Faber, 1990), 162–3.

Page 25: Meister Eckhart, "On Detachment," in *Meister Eckhart: Sermons and Treatises*, vol. 3, translated and edited by M. O'C. Walshe (Boston: Element Books, 1992), 120.

Page 25: Quoted in William A. Barry, *Finding God in All Things: A Companion to the Spiritual Exercises of St. Ignatius* (Notre Dame, Ind.: Ave Maria Press, 1991), 13–14.

Page 26: Annemarie Schimmel, trans., *Look! This Is Love: Poems of Rumi* (Boston: Shambhala Publications, 1996), 31. © 1991 by Annemarie Schimmel. Reprinted by arrangement with Shambhala Publications, Inc., Boston, www.shambhala.com

Page 26: From "Gandhi on Prayer," by Herrymon Maurer, in *Sacred Journey*, vol. 51, no. 1, Feb. 2000, 31.

Page 29: "Labor of Life," from *Shaker Music: Original Inspirational Hymns and Songs* (New York: William A. Pond & Co., 1884), 47.

Page 31: Abraham Joshua Heschel, *The Sabbath: Its Meaning for Modern Man* (New York: Farrar, Straus & Giroux, 1995), 100.

Page 33: "Love in the Morning," *Doubletake*, Winter 1996.

Page 37: Shams-ud-din Muhammad Hafiz, "Out of the Mouths of a Thousand Birds," from *The Subject Tonight is Love: Sixty Wild and Sweet Poems of Hafiz* (Myrtle Beach, S.C.: Pumpkin House Press, 1996), translation and copyright Daniel Ladinsky, 1996.

Page 39: Abraham Joshua Heschel, *The Insecurity of Freedom* (New York: Schocken Books, 1972), 258.

Page 41: Jim Forest, *Praying with Icons* (Maryknoll, N.Y.: Orbis Books, 1997), 45.

Page 43: Shunryu Suzuki, *Zen Mind, Beginner's Mind* (New York: Weatherhill, 1973), 26.

Page 43, bottom: Bonnie Myotai Treace, "Ancient Springtime Mind Light," in *Mountain Record*, XVII, No. 4, Summer 1999, 19.

Page 49: Thich Nhat Hanh, *Going Home: Jesus and Buddha as Brothers* (New York: Riverhead, 1999), 5.

Page 53: Shams-ud-din Muhammad Hafiz, "The Moon Is Also Busy," lines 1–3, in *I Heard God Laughing: Renderings of Hafiz* (Walnut Creek, Calif.: Sufism Reoriented, 1996), 37. Translation and copyright Daniel Ladinsky, 1996.

Page 61: Quoted in E. F. Morison, *St. Basil and His Rule: A Study in Early Monasticism* (New York: Oxford University Press, 1912), 60.

Page 63: Thich Nhat Hanh, *Going Home*, 9.

Page 71: John O'Donohue, *Eternal Echoes: Exploring Our Yearning to Belong* (New York: Cliff Street Books, 1999), 60–61.

Page 73: William Butler Yeats, "The Players Ask for a Blessing on the Psalteries and on Themselves," in *The Collected Poems of W. B. Yeats* (New York: Macmillan, 1956), 82.

Page 73: Shams-ud-din Muhammad Hafiz, "Cupping My Hands Like a Mountain Valley," lines 152–157, in *The Gift: Poems by Hafiz the Great Sufi Master* (New York: Penguin/Arkana, 1999), 267. Translation and copyright Daniel Ladinsky, 1996.

About SKYLIGHT PATHS Publishing

SkyLight Paths Publishing is creating a place where people of different spiritual traditions come together for challenge and inspiration, a place where we can help each other understand the mystery that lies at the heart of our existence.

Through spirituality, our religious beliefs are increasingly becoming a part of our lives—rather than *apart* from our lives. While many of us may be more interested than ever in spiritual growth, we may be less firmly planted in traditional religion. Yet, we do want to deepen our relationship to the sacred, to learn from our own as well as from other faith traditions, and to practice in new ways.

SkyLight Paths sees both believers and seekers as a community that increasingly transcends traditional boundaries of religion and denomination—people wanting to learn from each other, *walking together, finding the way.*

We at SkyLight Paths take great care to produce beautiful books that present meaningful spiritual content in a form that reflects the art of making high quality books. Therefore, we want to acknowledge those who contributed to the production of this book.

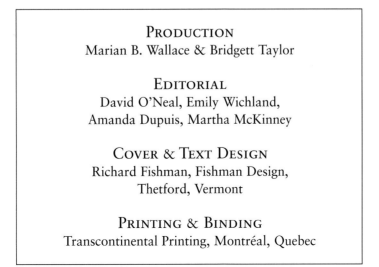

PRODUCTION
Marian B. Wallace & Bridgett Taylor

EDITORIAL
David O'Neal, Emily Wichland,
Amanda Dupuis, Martha McKinney

COVER & TEXT DESIGN
Richard Fishman, Fishman Design,
Thetford, Vermont

PRINTING & BINDING
Transcontinental Printing, Montréal, Quebec

AVAILABLE FROM BETTER BOOKSTORES.
TRY YOUR BOOKSTORE FIRST.

Other Interesting Books—Spirituality

Show Me Your Way
The Complete Guide to Exploring Interfaith Spiritual Direction
by *Howard A. Addison*

The rediscovery of an ancient spiritual practice— reimagined for the modern seeker.

This revealing book introduces people of all faiths—even those with no particular religious involvement—to the concept and practice of spiritual direction and, for the first time, to the dynamics of *interfaith* spiritual direction. Explores how spiritual direction differs within each major religious tradition, and how and where to find guidance within your faith community or beyond it. You really can gain spiritual inspiration from other faiths—*without leaving your own*.
5½ x 8½, 208 pp, HC, ISBN 1-893361-12-8 **$21.95**

Waking Up: *A Week Inside a Zen Monastery*
by *Jack Maguire*; Foreword by *John Daido Loori, Roshi*

An essential guide to what it's like to spend a week inside a Zen Buddhist monastery.

The notion of spending days at a time in silence and meditation amid the serene beauty of a Zen monastery may be appealing—but how do you do it, and what can you really expect from the experience? This essential guide provides the answers for everyone who's just curious, as well as for those who have dreamed of actually giving it a try and want to know where to begin.
6 x 9, 224 pp, b/w photographs, HC, ISBN 1-893361-13-6 **$21.95**

Making a Heart for God: *A Week Inside a Catholic Monastery*
by *Dianne Aprile*; Foreword by *Brother Patrick Hart, O.C.S.O.*

The essential guide to experiencing life in a Catholic monastery.

The second book in the "Week Inside" series looks at life inside a Catholic monastery, taking us to the Abbey of Gethsemani—the Trappist monastery in Kentucky that was home to author Thomas Merton—to explore the details: the work, meals, living arrangements, hours spent in prayer, and services that make up the structure of every day. For all those who are simply curious, as well as for anyone who is ready to pack their bag and try the monastic experience firsthand.
6 x 9, 208 pp, b/w photographs, HC, ISBN 1-893361-14-4 **$21.95**

Or phone, fax or mail to: SKYLIGHT PATHS Publishing
Sunset Farm Offices, Route 4 • P.O. Box 237 • Woodstock, Vermont 05091
Tel: (802) 457-4000   Fax: (802) 457-4004   www.skylightpaths.com
Credit card orders (800) 962-4544 (9AM–5PM ET Monday–Friday)
Generous discounts on quantity orders. Satisfaction guaranteed. Prices subject to change.

Spirituality

Who Is My God?
An Innovative Guide to Finding Your Spiritual Identity
Created by *the Editors at SkyLight Paths*

Spiritual Type™ + Tradition Indicator = Spiritual Identity

Your Spiritual Identity is an undeniable part of who you are—whether you've thought much about it or not. This dynamic resource provides a helpful framework to begin or deepen your spiritual growth. Start by taking the unique Spiritual Identity Self-Test™; tabulate your results; then explore one, two or more of twenty-eight faiths/spiritual paths followed in America today. "An innovative and entertaining way to think—and rethink—about your own spiritual path, or perhaps even to find one." —*Dan Wakefield,* author of *How Do We Know When It's God?*

6 x 9, 160 pp, Quality PB Original, ISBN 1-893361-08-X **$15.95**

Spiritual Manifestos
Visions for Renewed Religious Life in America from Young Spiritual Leaders of Many Faiths
Edited by *Niles Elliot Goldstein*; Preface by *Martin E. Marty*

Discover the reasons why so many people have kept organized religion at arm's length.

Here, ten young spiritual leaders, most in their mid-thirties, representing the spectrum of religious traditions—Protestant, Catholic, Jewish, Buddhist, Unitarian Universalist—present the innovative ways they are transforming our spiritual communities and our lives. "These ten articulate young spiritual leaders engender hope for the vitality of 21st-century religion." —*Forrest Church,* Minister of All Souls Church in New York City

6 x 9, 256 pp, HC, ISBN 1-893361-09-8 **$21.95**

The Art of Public Prayer: *Not for Clergy Only,* 2nd Edition
by *Lawrence A. Hoffman*

A resource for worshipers today looking to change hardened worship patterns that stand in the way of everyday spirituality.

Written for laypeople and clergy of any denomination, this ecumenical introduction to meaningful public prayer is for everyone who cares about religion today.

6 x 9, 288 pp, Quality PB, ISBN 1-893361-06-3 **$17.95**

Spirituality

Three Gates to Meditation Practice
A Personal Journey into Sufism, Buddhism, and Judaism
by *David A. Cooper*

Shows us how practicing within more than one spiritual tradition can lead us to our true home.

Here are over fifteen years from the journey of "post-denominational rabbi" David A. Cooper, author of *God Is a Verb*, and his wife, Shoshana—years in which the Coopers explored a rich variety of practices, from chanting Sufi *dhikr* to Buddhist Vipassanā meditation, to the study of kabbalah and esoteric Judaism. Their experience demonstrates that the spiritual path is really completely within our reach, whoever we are, whatever we do—as long as we are willing to practice it.

5½ x 8½, 240 pp, Quality PB, ISBN 1-893361-22-5 **$16.95**

Praying with Our Hands
Twenty-One Practices of Embodied Prayer from the World's Spiritual Traditions
by *Jon M. Sweeney*; Photographs by *Jennifer J. Wilson*;
Foreword by *Mother Tessa Bielecki*; Afterword by *Taitetsu Unno, Ph.D.*

A spiritual guidebook for bringing prayer into our bodies.

What gives our prayers meaning? How can we carry a prayerful spirit throughout our everyday lives? This inspiring book of reflections and accompanying photographs shows us twenty-one simple ways of using our hands to speak to God, to enrich our devotion and ritual. All express the various approaches of the world's religious traditions to bringing the body into worship. Spiritual traditions represented include Anglican, Sufi, Zen, Roman Catholic, Yoga, Shaker, Hindu, Jewish, Pentecostal, Eastern Orthodox, and many others.

8 x 8, 96 pp, 22 duotone photographs, Quality PB Original, ISBN 1-893361-16-0 **$16.95**

Labyrinths from the Outside In
Walking to Spiritual Insight—a Beginner's Guide
by *Donna Schaper* & *Carole Ann Camp*

The user-friendly, interfaith guide to making and using labyrinths— for meditation, prayer, and celebration.

Labyrinth walking is a spiritual exercise *anyone* can do. And it's rare among such practices in that it can be done by people together, regardless of their religious backgrounds or lack thereof. This accessible guide unlocks the mysteries of the labyrinth for all of us, providing ideas for using the labyrinth walk for prayer, meditation, and celebrations to mark the most important moments in life. Includes instructions for making a labyrinth of your own and finding one in your area.

6 x 9, 208 pp, b/w illus. and photographs, Quality PB Original, ISBN 1-893361-18-7 **$16.95**

Spirituality

One God Clapping: *The Spiritual Path of a Zen Rabbi*

by *Alan Lew* & *Sherril Jaffe*

The firsthand account of a spiritual journey from Zen Buddhist practitioner to rabbi.

A fascinating personal story of a Jewish meditation expert's roundabout spiritual journey from Zen Buddhist practitioner to rabbi. An insightful source of inspiration for each of us who is on the journey to find God in today's multi-faceted spiritual world.

5½ x 8½, 336 pp, Quality PB, ISBN 1-58023-115-2 **$16.95** (Available Feb. 2001)

Zen Effects: *The Life of Alan Watts*

by *Monica Furlong*

The first and only full-length biography of one of the most charismatic spiritual leaders of the twentieth century—now back in print!

Through his widely popular books and lectures, Alan Watts (1915–1973) did more to introduce Eastern philosophy and religion to Western minds than any figure before or since. Here is the only biography of this charismatic figure, who served as Zen teacher, Anglican priest, lecturer, academic, entertainer, a leader of the San Francisco renaissance, and author of more than 30 books, including *The Way of Zen, Psychotherapy East and West* and *The Spirit of Zen.*

6 x 9, 272 pp, Quality PB, ISBN 1-893361-32-2 **$16.95** (Available Feb. 2001)

The Way Into Jewish Mystical Tradition

by *Lawrence Kushner*

Explains the principles of Jewish mystical thinking, their religious and spiritual significance, and how they relate to our lives. A book that allows us to experience and understand the Jewish mystical approach to our place in the world.

6 x 9, 176 pp, HC, ISBN 1-58023-029-6 **$21.95**

The New Millennium Spiritual Journey

Change Your Life—
Develop Your Spiritual Priorities with Help from Today's Most Inspiring Spiritual Teachers

Created by *the Editors at SkyLight Paths*

A life-changing resource for reimagining your spiritual life.

Set your own course of reflection and spiritual transformation with the help of self-tests, spirituality exercises, sacred texts from many traditions, time capsule pages, and helpful suggestions from more than 20 spiritual teachers, including Karen Armstrong, Sylvia Boorstein and Dr. Andrew Weil.

7 x 9, 144 pp, Quality PB Original, ISBN 1-893361-05-5 **$16.95**

Spirituality

Honey from the Rock
An Introduction to Jewish Mysticism
by *Lawrence Kushner*

An insightful and absorbing introduction to the ten gates of Jewish mysticism and how it applies to daily life. "The easiest introduction to Jewish mysticism you can read."
6 x 9, 176 pp, Quality PB, ISBN 1-58023-073-3 **$15.95**

Eyes Remade for Wonder
The Way of Jewish Mysticism and Sacred Living
A Lawrence Kushner Reader

Intro. by *Thomas Moore*, author of *Care of the Soul*

Whether you are new to Kushner or a devoted fan, you'll find inspiration here. With samplings from each of Kushner's works, and a generous amount of new material, this book is to be read and reread, each time discovering deeper layers of meaning in our lives.
6 x 9, 240 pp, Quality PB, ISBN 1-58023-042-3 **$16.95**; HC, ISBN 1-58023-014-8 **$23.95**

Invisible Lines of Connection
Sacred Stories of the Ordinary
by *Lawrence Kushner* AWARD WINNER!

Through his everyday encounters with family, friends, colleagues and strangers, Kushner takes us deeply into our lives, finding flashes of spiritual insight in the process.
5½ x 8½, 160 pp, Quality PB, ISBN 1-879045-98-2 **$15.95**; HC, ISBN 1-879045-52-4 **$21.95**

Finding Joy
A Practical Spiritual Guide to Happiness
by *Dannel I. Schwartz* with *Mark Hass* AWARD WINNER!

Explains how to find joy through a time-honored, creative—and surprisingly practical—approach based on the teachings of Jewish mysticism and Kabbalah.
6 x 9, 192 pp, Quality PB, ISBN 1-58023-009-1 **$14.95**; HC, ISBN 1-879045-53-2 **$19.95**

Ancient Secrets
Using the Stories of the Bible to Improve Our Everyday Lives
by *Rabbi Levi Meier, Ph.D.* AWARD WINNER!

Drawing on a broad range of wisdom writings, distinguished rabbi and psychologist Levi Meier takes a thoughtful, wise and fresh approach to showing us how to apply the stories of the Bible to our everyday lives.
5½ x 8½, 288 pp, Quality PB, ISBN 1-58023-064-4 **$16.95**

Spirituality

A Heart of Stillness
A Complete Guide to Learning the Art of Meditation
by *David A. Cooper*

The only complete, nonsectarian guide to meditation, from one of our most respected spiritual teachers.

Experience what mystics have experienced for thousands of years. *A Heart of Stillness* helps you acquire on your own, with minimal guidance, the skills of various styles of meditation. Draws upon the wisdom teachings of Christianity, Judaism, Buddhism, Hinduism, and Islam as it teaches you the processes of purification, concentration, and mastery in detail.
5½ x 8½, 272 pp, Quality PB, ISBN 1-893361-03-9 **$16.95**

Silence, Simplicity & Solitude
A Complete Guide to Spiritual Retreat at Home
by *David A. Cooper*

The classic personal spiritual retreat guide that enables readers to create their own self-guided spiritual retreat at home.

Award-winning author David Cooper traces personal mystical retreat in all of the world's major traditions, describing the varieties of spiritual practices for modern spiritual seekers. Cooper shares the techniques and practices that encompass the personal spiritual retreat experience, allowing readers to enhance their meditation practices and create an effective, self-guided spiritual retreat in their own homes—without the instruction of a meditation teacher.
5½ x 8½, 336 pp, Quality PB, ISBN 1-893361-04-7 **$16.95**

God Whispers
Stories of the Soul, Lessons of the Heart
by *Rabbi Karyn D. Kedar*
6 x 9, 176 pp, Quality PB, ISBN 1-58023-088-1 **$15.95**

The Empty Chair: *Finding Hope and Joy—*
Timeless Wisdom from a Hasidic Master, Rebbe Nachman of Breslov AWARD WINNER!
Adapted by *Moshe Mykoff* and the *Breslov Research Institute*
4 x 6, 128 pp, Deluxe PB, 2-color text, ISBN 1-879045-67-2 **$9.95**

The Gentle Weapon: *Prayers for Everyday and Not-So-Everyday Moments*
Adapted from the Wisdom of Rebbe Nachman of Breslov by *Moshe Mykoff* and
S. C. Mizrahi, with the *Breslov Research Institute*
4 x 6, 144 pp, Deluxe PB, 2-color text, ISBN 1-58023-022-9 **$9.95**

Children's Spirituality

ENDORSED BY CATHOLIC, PROTESTANT, JEWISH, AND BUDDHIST RELIGIOUS LEADERS

Becoming Me
A Story of Creation
by *Martin Boroson*
Full-color illus. by *Christopher Gilvan-Cartwright*
NONDENOMINATIONAL, NONSECTARIAN
Told in the personal "voice" of the Creator, here is a story about creation and relationship that is about each one of us. In simple words and with radiant illustrations, the Creator tells an intimate story about love, about friendship and playing, about our world—and about ourselves. And with each turn of the page, we're reminded that we just might be closer to our Creator than we think! One Spirit Book Club Selection.
Ages 4 & up; 8 x 10, 32 pp, Full-color illus., HC, ISBN 1-893361-11-X **$16.95**

A Prayer for the Earth
The Story of Naamah, Noah's Wife
by *Sandy Eisenberg Sasso*
Full-color illus. by *Bethanne Andersen*
NONDENOMINATIONAL, NONSECTARIAN
This new story, based on an ancient text, opens children's religious imaginations to new ideas about the well-known story of the Flood. When God tells Noah to bring the animals of the world onto the ark, God also calls on Naamah, Noah's wife, to save each plant on Earth.
"A lovely tale. . . . Children of all ages should be drawn to this parable for our times."
—*Tomie de Paola*, artist/author of books for children
Ages 4 & up; 9 x 12, 32 pp, HC, Full-color illus., ISBN 1-879045-60-5 **$16.95**

The 11th Commandment
Wisdom from Our Children
by *The Children of America*
MULTICULTURAL, NONDENOMINATIONAL, NONSECTARIAN
"If there were an Eleventh Commandment, what would it be?" Children of many religious denominations across America answer this question—in their own drawings and words. From "No polluting the world," to "You shall not make fun of the handicapped," to "No punching in the head," this book helps us take a fresh look at how we can create a better world to live in. "A rare book of spiritual celebration for all people, of all ages, for all time."
—Bookviews
For all ages; 8 x 10, 48 pp, HC, Full-color illus., ISBN 1-879045-46-X **$16.95**

Children's Spirituality

In Our Image
God's First Creatures
by *Nancy Sohn Swartz*
Full-color illus. by *Melanie Hall*

A playful new twist on the Creation story—from the perspective of the animals. Celebrates the interconnectedness of nature and the harmony of all living things. "The vibrantly colored illustrations nearly leap off the page in this delightful interpretation." —*School Library Journal*
"A message all children should hear, presented in words and pictures that children will find irresistible." —*Rabbi Harold Kushner*, author of *When Bad Things Happen to Good People*
Ages 4 & up; 9 x 12, 32 pp, HC, Full-color illus., ISBN 1-879045-99-0 **$16.95**

God's Paintbrush
by *Sandy Eisenberg Sasso*; Full-color illus. by *Annette Compton*

Invites children of all faiths and backgrounds to encounter God openly in their own lives. Wonderfully interactive; provides questions adult and child can explore together at the end of each episode. "An excellent way to honor the imaginative breadth and depth of the spiritual life of the young." —*Dr. Robert Coles*, Harvard University
Ages 4 & up: 11 x 8½, 32 pp, HC, Full-color illus., ISBN 1-879045-22-2 **$16.95**

Also available: **A Teacher's Guide**
8½ x 11, 32 pp, PB, ISBN 1-879045-57-5 **$6.95**

God's Paintbrush Celebration Kit

Inspired by *God's Paintbrush*, now children can study, play and learn with this innovative classroom resource! Includes the use of crafts, games and other indoor and outdoor activities that invite children to think about God in new and exciting ways.
Ideal for ages 5–8; 9½ x 12, HC, Includes 5 sessions/40 full-color Activity Sheets and Teacher Folder with complete instructions. ISBN 1-58023-050-4 **$21.95**

In God's Name
by *Sandy Eisenberg Sasso*; Full-color illus. by *Phoebe Stone*

Like an ancient myth in its poetic text and vibrant illustrations, this award-winning modern fable about the search for God's name celebrates the diversity and, at the same time, the unity of all the people of the world. "What a lovely, healing book!" —*Madeleine L'Engle*
Ages 4 & up; 9 x 12, 32 pp, HC, Full-color illus., ISBN 1-879045-26-5 **$16.95**

Children's Spirituality

ENDORSED BY CATHOLIC, PROTESTANT, JEWISH, AND BUDDHIST RELIGIOUS LEADERS

Because Nothing Looks Like God

by *Lawrence and Karen Kushner*
Full-color illus. by *Dawn W. Majewski*

A vibrant way for children—and their adults— to explore what, where, and how God is in our lives.

MULTICULTURAL, NONDENOMINATIONAL, NONSECTARIAN

What is God like? The first collaborative work by husband-and-wife team Lawrence and Karen Kushner introduces children to the possibilities of spiritual life with three poetic spiritual stories. Real-life examples of happiness and sadness—from goodnight stories, to the hope and fear felt the first time at bat, to the closing moments of life—invite us to explore, together with our children, the questions we all have about God, no matter what our age.
Ages 4 & up; 11 x 8½, 32 pp, HC, Full-color illus., ISBN 1-58023-092-X **$16.95**

Where Is God? (A Board Book)

by *Lawrence and Karen Kushner*; Full-color illus. by *Dawn W. Majewski*

A gentle way for young children to explore how God is with us every day, in every way.

To young children the world is full of things to see and touch. This enchanting book gently invites children to become aware of God's presence all around them. Abridged from *Because Nothing Looks Like God* by Lawrence and Karen Kushner, *Where Is God?* has been specially adapted to board book format to delight and inspire young readers.
Ages 0–4; 5 x 5, 24 pp, Board, Full-color illus., ISBN 1-893361-17-9 **$7.95**

What Is God's Name? (A Board Book)

Everyone and everything in the world has a name. What is God's name?

by *Sandy Eisenberg Sasso*; Full-color illus. by *Phoebe Stone*

Each child begins to formulate an image for God in their preschool years, often one dominant image they keep for a lifetime…"shepherd," "mother," "father," "friend." In this simple, beautiful abridged version of Sasso's award-winning *In God's Name*, children see and hear the many names people have for God, and learn that each name is equal to the others and that God is One.
Ages 0–4; 5 x 5, 24 pp, Board, Full-color illus., ISBN 1-893361-10-1 **$7.95**

Children's Spirituality

God Said Amen

by *Sandy Eisenberg Sasso*
Full-color illus. by *Avi Katz*
MULTICULTURAL, NONDENOMINATIONAL, NONSECTARIAN

A warm and inspiring tale of two kingdoms: Midnight Kingdom is overflowing with water but has no oil to light its lamps; Desert Kingdom is blessed with oil but has no water to grow its gardens. The kingdoms' rulers ask God for help but are too stubborn to ask each other. It takes a minstrel, a pair of royal riding-birds and their young keepers, and a simple act of kindness to show that they need only reach out to each other to find the answers to their prayers.
Ages 4 & up; 9 x 12, 32 pp, HC, Full-color illus., ISBN 1-58023-080-6 **$16.95**

For Heaven's Sake

by *Sandy Eisenberg Sasso*; Full-color illus. by *Kathryn Kunz Finney*

Everyone talked about heaven: "Thank heavens." "Heaven forbid." "For heaven's sake, Isaiah." But no one would say what heaven was or how to find it. So Isaiah decides to find out, by seeking answers from many different people. "This book is a reminder of how well Sandy Sasso knows the minds of children. But it may surprise—and delight—readers to find how well she knows us grown-ups too." —*Maria Harris*, National Consultant in Religious Education, and author of *Teaching and Religious Imagination*
Ages 4 & up; 9 x 12, 32 pp, HC, Full-color illus., ISBN 1-58023-054-7 **$16.95**

But God Remembered
Stories of Women from Creation to the Promised Land

by *Sandy Eisenberg Sasso*; Full-color illus. by *Bethanne Andersen*

A fascinating collection of four different stories of women only briefly mentioned in biblical tradition and religious texts. Award-winning author Sasso vibrantly brings to life courageous and strong women from ancient tradition; all teach important values through their actions and faith. "Exquisite. . . . A book of beauty, strength and spirituality." —*Association of Bible Teachers*
Ages 7 & up; 9 x 12, 32 pp, HC, Full-color illus., ISBN 1-879045-43-5 **$16.95**

God in Between

by *Sandy Eisenberg Sasso*; Full-color illus. by *Sally Sweetland*

If you wanted to find God, where would you look? A magical, mythical tale that teaches that God can be found where we are: within all of us and the relationships between us. "This happy and wondrous book takes our children on a sweet and holy journey into God's presence." —*Rabbi Wayne Dosick, Ph.D.*, author of *The Business Bible* and *Soul Judaism*
Ages 4 & up; 9 x 12, 32 pp, HC, Full-color illus., ISBN 1-879045-86-9 **$16.95**

AVAILABLE FROM BETTER BOOKSTORES.
TRY YOUR BOOKSTORE FIRST.

Other Interesting Books—Spirituality

How to Be a Perfect Stranger, In 2 Volumes
A Guide to Etiquette in Other People's Religious Ceremonies
Ed. by *Stuart M. Matlins & Arthur J. Magida* **AWARD WINNER!**

Explains the rituals and celebrations of North America's major religions/denominations, helping an interested guest to feel comfortable, participate to the fullest extent possible, and avoid violating anyone's religious principles. Answers practical questions from the perspective of *any* other faith.

VOL. 1: North America's Largest Faiths
VOL. 1 COVERS: Assemblies of God • Baptist • Buddhist • Christian Church (Disciples of Christ) • Christian Science • Churches of Christ • Episcopalian/Anglican • Greek Orthodox • Hindu • Islam • Jehovah's Witnesses • Jewish • Lutheran • Methodist • Mormon • Presbyterian • Quaker • Roman Catholic • Seventh-day Adventist • United Church of Canada • United Church of Christ
6 x 9, 432 pp, Quality PB, ISBN 1-893361-01-2 **$19.95**

Vol. 2: More Faiths in North America
VOL. 2 COVERS: African American Methodist Churches • Baha'i • Christian and Missionary Alliance • Christian Congregation • Church of the Brethren • Church of the Nazarene • Evangelical Free Church • International Church of the Foursquare Gospel • International Pentecostal Holiness Church • Mennonite/Amish • Native American/First Nations • Orthodox Churches • Pentecostal Church of God • Reformed Church • Sikh • Unitarian Universalist • Wesleyan
6 x 9, 416 pp, Quality PB, ISBN 1-893361-02-0 **$19.95**

Prayer for People Who Think Too Much
A Guide to Everyday, Anywhere Prayer from the World's Faith Traditions
by *Mitch Finley*
Helps us make prayer a natural part of daily living.
Takes a thoughtful look at how each major faith tradition incorporates prayer into *daily* life. Explores Christian sacraments, Jewish holy days, Muslim daily prayer, "mindfulness" in Buddhism, and more, to help you better understand and enhance your own prayer practices. "I love this book." —*Caroline Myss,* author of *Anatomy of the Spirit*
5½ x 8½, 224 pp, Quality PB, ISBN 1-893361-21-7 **$16.95**; HC, ISBN 1-893361-00-4 **$21.95**

Or phone, fax or mail to: **SKYLIGHT PATHS** Publishing
Sunset Farm Offices, Route 4 • P.O. Box 237 • Woodstock, Vermont 05091
Tel: (802) 457-4000   Fax: (802) 457-4004 www.skylightpaths.com
Credit card orders (800) **962-4544** (9AM–5PM ET Monday–Friday)
Generous discounts on quantity orders. Satisfaction guaranteed. Prices subject to change.